AF381335

THE BEATLES

The Sound of the Sixties

Written by Florian Babusiaux
Translated by Rebecca Neal

History 50MINUTES.com

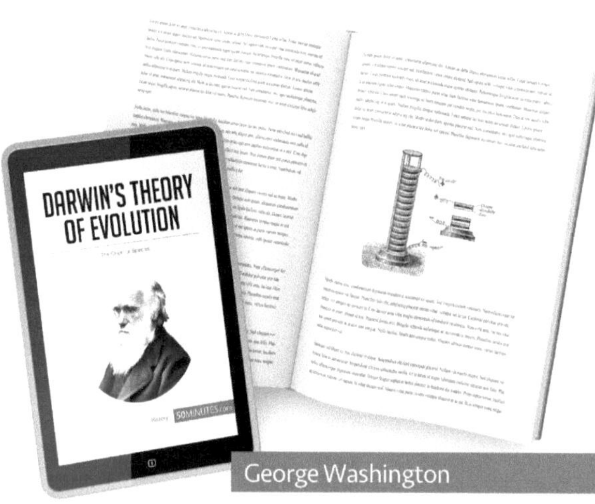

50MINUTES.com

BECOME AN EXPERT
IN HISTORY

George Washington

The Battle of Austerlitz

Neil Armstrong

The Six-Day War

The Fall of Constantinople

www.50minutes.com

THE BEATLES

KEY INFORMATION

- **Members:**
  - <u>John Lennon</u> (born 9 October 1940 in Liverpool, died 8 December 1980 in New York).
  - <u>George Harrison</u> (born 25 February 1943 in Liverpool, died 29 November 2001 in Los Angeles).
  - <u>Paul McCartney</u> (born 18 June 1942 in Liverpool).
  - <u>Ringo Starr</u> (born 7 July 1940 in Liverpool).
- **Main achievements:** the Beatles were one of the greatest British pop rock groups of all time, and they have had a vast musical and cultural impact around the world. They are currently the bestselling group of all time, with an astonishing two billion albums sold worldwide.

INTRODUCTION

Nowadays, everyone has heard of the Beatles. From humble beginnings in Liverpool, the Fab Four rose to worldwide fame in the 1960s with hit songs including "Love Me Do" (1962), "From Me to You" (1963) and "All You Need Is Love" (1967). Their music came to define the decade, and their popularity shows no signs of fading even today.

The Beatles both reflected and helped drive the major social and cultural upheavals that were taking place around them. They were one of the first British acts to break America, wrote over 200 songs and remain the bestselling group of all time, with over two billion albums sold. They also pioneered new sounds in rock and new studio recording techniques. For example, they were the first musicians to hold concerts in stadiums and to feature reverse tape effects on their songs.

However, some other facts about the Beatles are far less well-known. For example, they did not always go by that name, they invented the concept of hidden tracks, and their influence stretched far beyond just the decade they were active and the music industry. In this guide, you will learn all this and more as we take you on a whirlwind tour of the 1960s and give you an insight into the group who changed the music industry forever.

BIOGRAPHY

The Beatles at New York's John F. Kennedy International Airport, 7 February 1964.

EARLY YEARS, FIRST MEETING AND MUSICAL DEBUT (1950S-1961)

John Lennon, George Harrison, Paul McCartney and Richard Starkey (better known as Ringo Starr) were all born and grew up in working-class families in Liverpool. George and Paul attended the same school, the Liverpool Institute, and became friends in their early teens. John, who was a couple of years older and went to a different school, did not meet them until the mid-1950s. Ringo left school between 1954 and 1955 and took on a series of odd jobs. At this stage, he had not yet met his future bandmates.

McCartney and Harrison met Lennon and joined the Quarrymen, his group at that time, in 1957 and 1958 respectively. Lennon was the group's lead vocalist, and also played guitar. The group's lineup gradually changed, and by 1960 only Lennon, McCartney (second guitar and vocals) and Harrison (lead guitar) were left. They were soon joined by Pete Best (British drummer, born in 1941) on drums and Stuart Sutcliffe (British musician and painter, 1940-1962) on bass. The group played a few local gigs in Liverpool and the surrounding towns, before being invited to play in clubs in Hamburg.

In Hamburg, the group experienced the city's nightlife and lived in poor conditions, but also learnt a lot, honed their skills and became friends with Ringo Starr, the drummer of Rory

Storm and the Hurricanes, another British group playing there.

THE MEANING OF THE GROUP'S NAME

Between 1958 and 1960, the group performed under several names, including Johnny and the Moondogs, the Rainbows, the Beetles, the Silver Beetles, Long John and the Silver Beatles, and the Silver Beats. It was not until the summer of 1960 that they settled on the Beatles, which combined the "beetles" of some of their previous names and the beat of rock music.

SUCCESS AND BEATLEMANIA (1962-1965)

By 1962, the group's members were Lennon (vocals and guitar), Harrison (lead guitar), McCartney (bass) and Starr (drums). Sutcliffe had decided to focus on art, his main passion, in 1961, while Best was dropped in favour of Starr in August 1962. With this lineup, the group released their first successful single, "Love Me Do".

The Beatles followed the advice of their new manager, Brian Epstein (1934-1967), and adopted a new look. Previously, they had donned pointed boots, jeans and leather jackets and worn their hair in Elvis Presley-style quiffs, but now they got bowl cuts and began wearing suits and ties.

The group's second single, "Please Please Me" (1963), topped the charts in Britain and gave them the chance to record their first album with the same name in February 1963.

This was followed by a string of hits, including "From Me to You", "I Want to Hold Your Hand" (1963) and "She Loves You" (1963), which made the group famous nationwide. In early 1964, they toured in the USA and met with great success. This marked the beginning of Beatlemania, as enthusiasts swarmed record stores to get their hands on the latest Beatles singles, teenage girls' screams drowned out the music at their concerts and some fans even fainted in their presence. From this point until 1967, all the group's singles and albums topped the charts, and they toured, produced albums and shot films and shows at a frenzied pace.

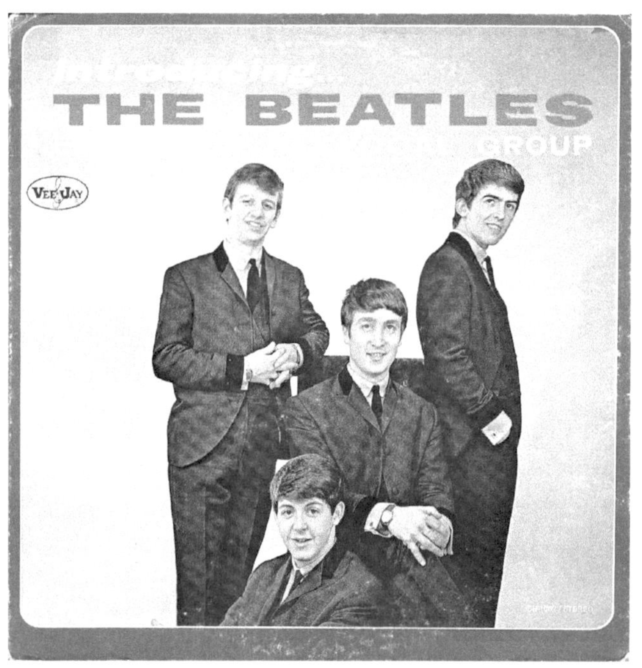

| Vinyl of *Introducing... The Beatles* (1964), the first Beatles album released in the USA.

RETURN TO THE STUDIO AND SPLIT (1966-1970)

By 1966, the Beatles were exhausted by the hysteria surrounding them, and decided to stop touring to focus on recording new music.

A RECORD-BREAKING GROUP

The group's concert at New York's Shea Stadium on 15 August 1965 drew a crowd of between 55 000 and 60 000 people, the largest audience ever for a music performance at that time. It was also the first time in the history of pop music that a group had played in a stadium.

The group began experimenting with increasingly innovative songs, deeper lyrics and more complex compositions. This period saw the release of iconic albums such as *Sgt. Pepper's Lonely Hearts Club Band* (1967) and *Abbey Road* (1969), which became landmarks in rock music.

THE BEATLES AND TELEVISION

In 1967, "All You Need Is Love", one of the Beatles' most famous singles, was released. On 25 June of that year, the group played it live on *Our World*, the first international satellite television programme. An estimated 350 million people tuned in to watch the performance live.

However, by 1968 tensions had appeared within the group. Lennon had a new girlfriend, the Japanese artist Yoko Ono (born in 1933), and kept bringing her with him to the studio, to the chagrin of his bandmates.

| John Lennon and Yoko Ono in Amsterdam, March 1969.

Moreover, all four bandmates seemed less and less happy to be part of the group. Indeed, Ringo Starr left the band for a few weeks before coming back in late 1968, and George Harrison did the same in early 1969. Then, after the recording of *Abbey Road*, Lennon announced that he was leaving the group.

The Beatles officially separated in 1970 and never got back together. Lennon was shot dead in 1980, while Harrison died of cancer in 2001. McCartney and Starr are both still alive, and have remained active in the music industry.

POLITICAL, SOCIAL AND ECONOMIC CONTEXT

The Beatles will always be closely associated with the 1960s: they got their first music contract in Hamburg and settled on their band name in 1960; they released their first album, *Please Please Me*, in 1963; and their last album, *Let It Be*, came out in 1970, which was also the year that the group split up. They were a product of their time, and both reflected and inspired the fashions of the decade.

From the bowl cuts they sported at the start of their career to the psychedelia of the late 1960s, the Beatles played a vital role in promoting a particular lifestyle and outlook around the world, and these later became inextricably tied to the 1960s in the popular imagination.

THE ADVENT OF THE CONSUMER SOCIETY

The period from 1946 to 1973 was a time of unprecedented growth in developed countries, and saw the development of the global economy and the beginnings of globalisation. This growth went hand in hand with the rise of mass consumption. Purchasing power tripled in developed countries, and households spent more and more on education, cars and leisure activities.

The numerous scientific advances of this time also influenced the emerging mass culture. For example, television broadcast major international events into people's living rooms, and virtually every household now had access to a radio set. The new technological possibilities and consumer society of the 1960s allowed the Beatles to reach more people than ever before and win over millions of new fans.

SEX, DRUGS, ROCK 'N' ROLL AND PROTESTS

In the 1960s, the Vietnam War (1954-1975) was at its height, and the first protests against the conflict began to take place in the USA. These protests took the form of demonstrations, general strikes or vast popular gatherings. At the Woodstock Festival in 1969, which attracted an unprecedented number of attendees and came to symbolise hippie culture, artists including Jimi Hendrix (American musician and singer, 1942-1970) made their opposition to the war clear. The Beatles, and John Lennon in particular, joined the anti-Vietnam War movement at the end of the decade.

Other protest movements at this time took aim at consumerism, which was decried as a way of imposing conformism and stifling individuality.

These various protest groups eventually gave rise to a counter-culture, and in the late 1960s the hippie movement appeared in the USA, before spreading to Europe. The early members of the movement, who were generally young people from affluent backgrounds, rejected social conventions, eschewed violence and advocated a return to nature and sexual liberation.

Hippies embraced so-called flower power, and tended to join together in communities bound by shared interests: musicians such as Bob Dylan (American songwriter, composer and singer, born in 1941) and Pink Floyd (British rock group, formed in 1965), hallucinogenic drugs and Eastern religion and philosophy. Consequently, Buddhism, yoga, meditation and mantras (sacred words or phrases repeated at a particular rhythm) came into fashion.

The Beatles also dabbled in this subculture, and their 1967 album *Sgt. Pepper's Lonely Hearts Club Band* is often considered an ode to the hippie movement. In early 1968, they travelled to India, where they immersed themselves in meditation. Harrison was the band member who was most influenced by Eastern philosophy and music.

Alongside these lifestyle philosophies, the mid-1960s onwards saw the development of another counter-culture movement: psychedelia. The adjective "psychedelic" is formed of "psyche" and the Greek *delos*, meaning "visible"; in other words, psychedelia makes the psyche visible. Enthusiasts wanted to alter their mental state, and sought to do this by taking hallucinogenic substances which heightened the individual's sensations and could trigger hallucinations. Taking these drugs allegedly helped users to travel within themselves and open their minds to deeper awareness.

The Beatles, particularly Lennon and Harrison, were frequent LSD users, as they believed that the drug would allow them to explore their inner selves. The band's drug use had a clear influence on the sound and lyrics of a number of their songs, particularly those produced between 1965 and 1967.

A DECADE OF UPHEAVAL

The 1960s, particularly the second half of the decade, was a period of artistic, cultural, scientific, technological, economic, sexual and moral revolution.

The decade was dominated by the musical tastes, clothing preferences and language of the young generation born during or just after the Second World War. The generational divide was thrown into even sharper relief with the emergence of the hippie movement. Young people wanted nothing to do with the values and mores of their parents' generation, particularly in terms of spirituality and sexuality, and tried instead to build a new world based on peace, love and a sense of community.

The Beatles were part of this generation and embodied its aspirations perfectly. As well as representing the values of their time, they also exerted an undeniable influence on the society and culture around them, and in most people's minds they are now inextricably linked to the 1960s.

HIGHLIGHTS

FORMATIVE YEARS IN LIVERPOOL AND HAMBURG

When the 15-year-old Paul McCartney met the 17-year-old John Lennon at a village fête in Woolton, on the outskirts of Liverpool, on 6 July 1957, there was no way he could have imagined that they would go on to write over 200 songs together and become two of the biggest celebrities on the planet. Likewise, George Harrison, who joined the band at the age of just 14 after auditioning for Lennon in an empty double-decker bus, must have had no idea of the fame and success that awaited them.

However, the early days of their career were not all plain sailing. Although getting rich was never their goal, they wanted to be able to make a living from their music, but they earned practically nothing from their early gigs in Liverpool clubs such as the Jacaranda and the Cavern Club.

In August 1960, the group (which at that time

comprised Lennon, McCartney, Harrison, Sutcliffe and Best) were offered their first real contract by the talent manager Allan Williams (1930-2016), the owner of one of the Liverpool clubs where they had played. This first "tour", which took them to the German city of Hamburg, saw them living in relatively difficult conditions. They often played from early evening to the small hours of the morning in clubs frequented by prostitutes, drunken sailors and aggressive military men, and lived in shabby accommodation. Indeed, sometimes they did not even have washing facilities, so they had to wash themselves in club toilets.

However, the Fab Four had only good things to say about their spell in Hamburg, which was a formative experience for them. It was also at this time that McCartney switched from guitar to bass (following the departure and then early death of Stuart Sutcliffe from an aneurysm in 1962) and the members of the group became friends with Ringo Starr, who ended up replacing Pete Best as drummer.

The Beatles made five trips to Hamburg between 1960 and 1962. The first of these lasted from August to November 1960, when George Harrison had to leave Germany as he was still a minor and did not have the right to work in the country. The band only returned to Germany in March 1961, once Harrison had turned 18. Their last stay in the country was in December 1962.

EPSTEIN, MARTIN AND "LOVE ME DO"

In 1961, the Beatles met the Liverpool record store owner Brian Epstein, who became their manager. It was Epstein who encouraged them to abandon their jeans and leather jackets in favour of suits, as he thought that this would improve their image and give them the opportunity to play in larger, more respectable venues. Epstein got in touch with record companies and worked hard to secure a recording contract for the group, but his early efforts were in vain.

George Martin (1926-2016), a producer at Parlophone, eventually gave them an audition. He saw the group's potential, but was less than impressed with their drummer, Pete Best. The other members therefore decided to replace him with Ringo Starr.

In September 1962, the Beatles recorded their first single, "Love Me Do". Although it only charted at number 17 in Britain, the group were happy with the amount of radio airplay it received. Their second single, "Please Please Me", came out in January of the following year and shot straight to the top of the charts. This success allowed the group to record their first full album, also called *Please Please Me*, which came out in March 1963.

This debut album spent seven months at the top of the charts and made the Beatles a household name across England. The group had two further number one singles in 1963, "From Me To You" and "She Loves You". With these songs, the group's fame spread through the rest of Europe, giving rise to what the British press dubbed "Beatlemania".

The Beatles also won people over with their trademark, sometimes borderline provocative humour. On 4 November 1963, they performed in front of the British royal family at the Prince of Wales Theatre in London. Before their last song, "Twist and Shout" (1963), Lennon said to the crowd: "For our last number I'd like to ask your help. The people in the cheaper seats clap your hands, and the rest of you if you'd just rattle your jewellery" (*The Beatles Anthology*, 2012: 105).

BREAKING AMERICA

It was not long before Beatlemania spread around the world, and the group soon became success-ful in the USA, which was home to their greatest musical influences: Chuck Berry (1926-2017), Elvis Presley (1935-1977), Buddy Holly (1936-1959) and Eddie Cochran (1938-1960), among others.

On 13 January 1964, the single "I Want to Hold Your Hand" was released in the USA. Its success (it reached number one in February) inspired the group to tour America. According to Lennon, they did not want to go to America until they had a number one single there, so that they knew they would not flop. The group touched down in New York on 7 February and were immediately mobbed by thousands of frenzied fans. A few days later, they played five songs on the popular variety show *The Ed Sullivan Show* and broke the programme's audience record, with some 73 million Americans tuning in to watch it live. This cemented the four boys from Liverpool's success in America.

They were the first British pop group to enjoy this level of success in the USA, paving the way for other British rock groups such as the Rolling Stones, the Kinks and the Who, which were formed in 1962, 1963 and 1964 respectively. Even now, the Beatles still hold the all-time album sales record in the USA, with almost 210 million albums sold.

WORLDWIDE SUCCESS

From this point onwards, the Beatles found themselves swept up in a whirlwind that showed no sign of slowing down. Between 1963 and 1966, they released seven albums, shot two films (*A Hard Day's Night*, 1964 and *Help!*, 1965) and went on multiple world tours.

Each of their singles and albums shot to number one not only in Britain, but also in numerous other countries around the world. It was not until February 1967 that one of their records, the double A-side single "Strawberry Fields Forever"/"Penny Lane", only reached number two in Britain, although it was still number one in the USA.

The group's global success can be most clearly seen with the 1965 single "Yesterday", which was composed, recorded and performed live by Paul McCartney, and appeared on the album *Help!*. It remains one of the most-played songs of all time, and has inspired almost 3000 official covers.

THE END OF TOURING, DRUGS AND AWARDS

1965 and 1966 were key years for the group. The albums *Rubber Soul* and *Revolver*, which, according to Harrison, could have been combined into a single album, marked a shift towards more philosophical, introspective lyrics. They were produced at a time when the Beatles were discovering marijuana alongside Bob Dylan, as well as LSD, which was legal at the time.

The use of these drugs steered the Beatles in a new direction, as their experiences with them inspired them to add new tones and sounds, as well as greater lyrical depth, to their music.

The Beatles discover LSD

John Lennon and George Harrison were the first Beatles to discover LSD, although they did so unknowingly. In April 1965, they were invited a mutual friend's house. After their meal, the friend, who was a dentist, slipped LSD into their coffees. This was a life-changing experience for the two men, especially Lennon, who became a heavy user of LSD. McCartney was the last member of the group to try the drug, in 1966.

Rubber Soul (1965) was the first Beatles album in which not every song is about women or love in some way. This can be seen in "Nowhere Man" (1965), an introspective song penned by John

Lennon. It was also the first album to abandon the conventions of rock 'n' roll, which the band had always adhered to up to that point in a bid to retain the support of their first fans, the ones who had listened to them play pure rock 'n' roll songs at clubs in Liverpool and Hamburg between 1960 and 1962.

This album was more personal and its songs formed more of a coherent whole than had been the case previously. The group maintained this new approach in their subsequent albums. They also gradually changed their look, letting their hair grow out and varying their outfits.

A CONTROVERSIAL DECORATION

In October 1965, all four members of the Beatles were awarded MBEs for their contribution to music and for the positive image of Britain that they promoted abroad. However, some other recipients, mainly veterans of the Second World War (1939-1945) and other military leaders, turned down their awards in protest at being honoured alongside pop singers.

1965 and 1966 were also significant because these were the years when the Beatles stopped touring. By this point, they were exhausted by Beatlemania and had had enough of the frenzied atmosphere at their concerts. Lennon said: "I reckon we could send out four waxwork dummies of ourselves and that would satisfy the crowds. Beatles concerts are nothing to do with music any more. They're just bloody tribal rites" (*ibid.*, p. 229).

The band had also grown frustrated at not being able to go anywhere without being mobbed by dozens of hysterical fans. Harrison later said: "The only place we ever got any peace was when we got in the suite and locked ourselves in the bathroom" (*ibid.*, p. 155).

Furthermore, some of the more experimental sounds and innovative recording techniques on *Rubber Soul* and *Revolver*, such as reverse tape effects, were impossible to replicate live. This was limiting for the group: they were forced to continue playing the rock 'n' roll songs that had made them famous, which must have made them feel that they had not moved on from Hamburg five years previously.

On 29 August 1966, the Beatles held what would be the penultimate concert of their career as a group in San Francisco (their last concert would be an improvised show on the roof of the building of their record label, Apple, on 30 January 1969). The group spent the following years in the studio, but remained as popular as ever.

THE FIRST CONCEPT ALBUM IN ROCK HISTORY?

In June 1967, the iconic album *Sgt. Pepper's Lonely Hearts Club Band* was released. This innovative concept album revolutionised the music industry, and is considered by some to be the greatest rock album of all time.

Sgt. Pepper's Lonely Hearts Club Band can be described as a concept album because it is not just a succession of distinct songs:

- The group tried to link songs together musically, with the end of one continuing seamlessly into the beginning of another.
- The entire album is based around the concept of another band, the eponymous Sgt. Pepper's Lonely Hearts Club Band, which plays an

entire set over the course of the album. This makes the album as a whole very coherent: the opening track introduces the band ("We're Sergeant Pepper's Lonely Hearts Club Band/ We hope you have enjoyed the show/Sergeant Pepper's Lonely Hearts Club Band/We're sorry but it's time to go"), while the penultimate track is a reprise of the first, but played faster and with a different tonality.

- The album sleeve was totally original: it could be opened up to reveal a plate with accessories that could be cut out and a transcription of the song lyrics.

A DIFFICULT PERIOD IN 1967

On 22 August 1967, at the end of the famous "Summer of Love", Brian Epstein, who had been the Beatles' manager since 1961, was found dead at his London home following a barbiturates overdose. The members of the group were left deeply shaken by his death and struggled to move on from it.

THE SUMMER OF LOVE

The summer of 1967 marked the high point of the hippie movement and became known as the Summer of Love. It originated with the Human Be-In, a spontaneous gathering of hippies in San Francisco's Haight-Ashbury neighbourhood on 14 January 1967 in which hundreds of people met up to share drugs and music. The event was covered extensively in the media.

A few months later, during the summer holidays, this success attracted almost 100 000 young people from all over the world to the same place. The gathering promised complete freedom, but as the neighbourhood was gradually overrun by sex, drugs and violence, the participants began to leave, bringing the Summer of Love to an end.

The album *Sgt. Pepper's Lonely Hearts Club Band* is considered to be one of the key symbols of this unprecedented event.

1967 also saw the release of the first film the group codirected, *Magical Mystery Tour*, and of an album with the same name. Unfortunately, the musical film was panned by critics, as the lack of colours did not do justice to the psychedelic dimension of their work. This negative reception is generally considered to be the Beatles' first failure.

During this period, the group's appearance was greatly influenced by the hippie movement: they grew out their hair, stopped shaving their beards and moustaches, and began wearing brightly coloured shirts, wide trousers and garish suits.

INDIA, "THE WHITE ALBUM" AND THE FIRST DISAGREEMENTS

The following year, attracted to the Eastern philosophies that were in vogue at the time, the Beatles spent several weeks in India with Maharishi Mahesh Yogi (1917-2008) in order to explore transcendental meditation more fully.

When they were not practising meditation with the Maharishi, the Beatles were writing new music. This was a very productive period for them: in the space of just a few weeks, they wrote over 40 songs. Many of these songs made it onto their next album, called simply *The Beatles* but more commonly known as the White Album because of its plain white cover.

| Cover of the White Album, 1968.

The recording of the album was not all plain sailing. By 1968, John Lennon and Yoko Ono were officially a couple, and Ono began spending more and more time in the studio. Until this point, no girlfriends had come between the four bandmates, but now things were becoming tense. Relations between the members became increasingly fraught, to such a point that Ringo Starr left the group for a few weeks before coming back in autumn 1968. The presence of other musicians, such as Eric Clapton (born in 1945) for the song "While My Guitar Gently Weeps" (1968), helped to paper over these tensions for a time.

ABBEY ROAD: THE CURTAIN CALL

However, there was no denying that relations between the bandmates were gradually deteriorating, and the discord worsened in January 1969. McCartney embarked on a project entitled "Get Back", which involved filming the band's rehearsals before they played live at the end of the film. They played around 100 songs, but the project ultimately came to nothing. Meanwhile, the rest of the group were finding it increasingly difficult to put up with Yoko Ono's now-constant presence in the studio.

McCartney's apparent need to control everything at all times was also beginning to wear on the other members. The documentary *The*

Beatles Anthology provides us with a glimpse of the project's atmosphere. A visibly exasperated George Harrison snaps at McCartney when he is trying to show him how to play a guitar riff, telling him sarcastically that he will do whatever he wants him to do. Harrison also left the group for a brief spell in January 1969, before returning shortly afterwards.

Finally, in August 1969 peace prevailed for long enough for the group to record *Abbey Road*, which remains one of the most famous pop rock albums of all time. Virtually everyone recognises the iconic cover, which is a photograph of the four men walking across a zebra crossing on the eponymous London street on 8 August 1969. A number of the album's songs allude to the band's difficulties. *Abbey Road* also features the songs "Here Comes the Sun" (1969) and "Something" (1969), which were written by Harrison, who until that point had simply been known as the group's guitarist rather than as a talented songwriter and composer. However, these tracks brought him recognition as Lennon and McCartney's equal in terms of songwriting and composing.

The Hidden Track

Abbey Road is also known for featuring what is considered to be the first hidden track in the history of rock music. "Her Majesty", which is sung by Paul McCartney and comes in at under 30 seconds, is not included on the album's track list. It comes 15 seconds after "The End", the last listed track.

The recording of this album was the last time the Fab Four were together in the studio. Once it was over, McCartney made a last-ditch attempt to renew their old chemistry by suggesting a tour of small venues. However, Lennon refused and announced that he was leaving the group for good. The news that the group had split was not made public until April 1970, by which time they had already been separated for months.

In spite of their split, another album, *Let It Be*, came out on 8 May 1970 in Britain. This, the group's 12th album, featured the tracks that had been recorded as part of McCartney's "Get Back" project at the start of the previous year. The album was produced by Phil Spector (born in

1939), with the consent of Lennon and Harrison. Spector modified the tracks somewhat, notably by adding new sound effects, but in spite of everything the album was a hit.

IMPACT

The group's music and the personalities of its four members undeniably had a major sociocultural impact.

THE BEATLES' MUSIC

It is hard to quantify the precise extent of the Beatles' impact on the music industry, but we can safely say that it is immense, given that it is still felt today, almost 50 years after the band's split.

Many celebrated groups and artists who were active at the same time as or after the Beatles have cited the band as a major influence. These include the Bee Gees (Australian-British pop group, formed in 1958), the Beach Boys (American pop group, formed in 1961), the Kinks, the Monkees (American pop rock group, formed in 1965), Pink Floyd, Genesis (British rock group, formed in 1967), Nirvana (American alternative rock group, formed in 1987), as well as David Bowie (British musician and singer, 1947-2016),

Prince (American artist, 1958-2016), Michael Jackson (American musician and singer, 1958-2009) and, more recently, Oasis (British rock group, formed in 1991) and Coldplay (British rock group, formed in 1996).

Although Lennon and McCartney were not the first singer-songwriters, they were largely responsible for popularising this trend. Before the Beatles, few successful pop acts wrote and composed their own songs; for example, only two of Elvis's songs were written by him.

The Beatles' musical impact extended to the recording industry as a whole, which they revolutionised. They redefined the album itself: rather than being a collection of songs, it became an artistic project, with the songs forming a coherent whole. The scope of the band's ambition first became clear in *Rubber Soul* and continued in their subsequent albums, while their eighth album, *Sgt. Pepper's Lonely Hearts Club Band*, pioneered the concept album.

IMPACT OUTSIDE MUSIC

During the 1960s

The Beatles also influenced the society around them, particularly the younger generation growing up after the war, throughout their careers. In terms of style, for example, many young people copied the famous mop top, which the Beatles sported from 1962 to 1965.

Their British sense of humour, as depicted in the film *A Hard Day's Night*, directed by Richard Lester (American director, born in 1932), bolstered their popularity among younger and older fans alike. Young people around the world thought that they were "cool" and saw them as role models with whom they could identify and whom they could try to emulate.

The group was at their most influential after 1965, after they stopped touring and their songs became more mature and reflective. They now used their music to spread the hippie ideals of peace and love ("All You Need Is Love"), to tell poetic stories ("Eleanor Rigby", 1966) and to encourage listeners to think about contemporary political issues ("Revolution", 1968).

Their lyrics, outlandish ways of dressing and introduction to Eastern philosophy shaped an entire generation. The group both influenced and were influenced by young people in the 1960s, and together they shattered the dogmas and strict moral values of the prewar generation.

The group's philosophy, poetry and way of life attracted many followers and provided a stark illustration of the break with the prewar world. The Beatles embodied the way young people in the 1960s were rejecting the strict morals and conformism that characterised their parents' generation. Young people at this time had different concerns, sought out new experiences and viewed life and the society around them differently, and this was reflected by the Beatles and a number of other contemporary artists.

After the 1960s

The Beatles were frequently parodied on television, whether by comedians during their shows or during comedy series. The group's history, music and lifestyle have also been the subject of films such as *I Wanna Hold Your Hand* (1978) by Robert Zemeckis (American director, producer and scriptwriter, born in 1952) and the musical *Across the Universe* (2007) by Julie Taymor (American director and filmmaker, born in 1952).

In 2006, Cirque du Soleil launched a permanent show called The Beatles LOVE, which features dances and circus skills performed to the group's music. For example, the song "Lucy in the Sky with Diamonds" (1967) features an aerial performance by a trapeze artist, who represents Lucy in the song. The Beatles LOVE proved a great success, and is far from the only show to make use of the group's songs.

Their popularity shows no signs of waning: in 2009 a video game, *The Beatles: Rock Band* was released to acclaim from both the press and ordinary gamers. The group remains popular with young people today, and their songs are downloaded in huge numbers.

POLITICAL AND ECONOMIC IMPACT

The Beatles stood with the hippie movement in opposing British participation in the Vietnam War. In 1969, Lennon even went so far as to return his MBE in protest at Britain's involvement in Southeast Asia.

Although they were not overly vocal about their political beliefs in their music, some of the Beatles' songs, such as "Piggies" (1968), contained anti-establishment criticism, while others, such as "Revolution", invited contemporary listeners to think about revolutions that were taking place in the world at that time.

The Beatles also took a stand against racial segregation, which was current practice in the USA and South Africa at that time. For example, they refused to perform in certain countries because they believed that apartheid should not be condoned, and in January 1970 Lennon made a donation to London's black community. These kinds of gestures were important because of their potential impact on the group's sizeable fanbase.

Finally, the Beatles' success brought major long-term economic benefits to Liverpool, the city where they were born. Even in 2016, 1% of all jobs in Liverpool were linked either directly or indirectly to the Beatles. A Beatles museum opened in 1990, and there are guided tours to visit places made famous by their songs or by their connection to the group, such as the Cavern Club, Penny Lane, Strawberry Fields and the houses where John and Paul grew up. Finally, the International Beatleweek Festival takes place every August and sees dozens of groups from all over the world play John, Paul, George and Ringo's greatest hits in front of thousands of fans. The city has benefitted hugely from the money and jobs that result from this influx of visitors.

SUMMARY

- The Beatles were a British pop rock group, originally from Liverpool. The band's definitive lineup was John Lennon, Paul McCartney, George Harrison and Ringo Starr. Their career took off in 1962, with the recording and release of their first single, "Love Me Do".
- Their first two albums and their successful US tour at the start of 1964, which made it possible for other British acts to break into the American market, triggered the frenzied enthusiasm that the British press dubbed "Beatlemania".
- 1964 and 1965 were the group's most prolific years: they released four albums, starred in two films and toured the world. However, the more their popularity grew, the more challenging their tours and concerts became: as sound systems were still relatively primitive at this time, the screams of their teenage fans drowned out their music. Furthermore, the four young men could not go anywhere without being mobbed by legions of fans.

- Consequently, the group decided to stop touring in 1966, and from then on spent most of their time in the studio. They used new sounds and recording techniques to create innovative songs, and their lyrics became more profound and less focused on love and women.
- The group began to experiment with drugs, which subsequently influenced their music. That said, they did not overtly advocate drug use.
- They also dabbled in psychedelia, as can be seen on the album *Sgt. Pepper's Lonely Hearts Club Band*. They adopted the ideas of the hippie movement, thus helping to popularise it and its philosophy around the world.
- Although they continued to make chart-topping songs and albums together, tensions appeared from 1968 onwards, partly as a result of the arrival of Yoko Ono, who was seen as an intruder in the world that had previously been shared by the four of them. These tensions meant that they were less and less enthusiastic about playing together, and the bonds between the bandmates began to fray. In 1970, the group officially separated for good.
- By 1970, the world was not the same as it had

been ten years earlier. The Beatles had changed too: they were no longer clean-cut young men singing love songs, but a more unconventional group whose lyrics dealt with political and philosophical themes. The music of the Beatles is inextricably linked with the 1960s: the group was formed, grew up and fell apart in the course of this decade. Their music won them fans all over the world and had a lasting impact on society and the recording industry. It is therefore not an exaggeration to say that their songs are the soundtrack to the sixties.

We want to hear from you!
Leave a comment on your online library
and share your favourite books on social media!

FIND OUT MORE

BIBLIOGRAPHY

- Guesdon, J-M. and Margotin, P. (2013) *All the Songs: The Story Behind Every Beatles Release*. New York: Black Dog & Leventhal Publishers, Inc.

- Howlett, K. (2012) *The Beatles*. London: Apple Corps Ltd.

- Miles, B. (2012) *The Beatles Phenomenon: A Celebration in Words, Pictures and Music*. London: Omnibus Press.

- Plassat, F. (2011) *The Beatles Discomania*. Paris: Jbz & Cie.

- The Beatles (2012) *The Beatles Anthology*. San Francisco: Chronicle Books.

- Tillery, G. (2011) *Working Class Mystic: A Spiritual Biography of George Harrison*. Wheaton, Illinois: Quest Books.

- Weill, C. (2011) Les années 60 : dix ans qui ont changé le monde. *L'Obs*. [Online]. [Accessed 12 January 2018]. Available from: <https://www.nouvelobs.com/le-dossier-de-l-obs/20111221.OBS7280/les-annees-60-dix-ans-qui-ont-change-le-monde.html>

ADDITIONAL SOURCES

- Barrell, T. (2017) *The Beatles on the Roof.* London: Omnibus Press.

- Davies, H. (2009) *The Beatles: The Authorised Biography.* London: Ebury Press.

- Lewisohn, M. (1996) *The Complete Beatles Chronicle.* Vacaville, California: Bounty Books.

- MacDonald, I. (2008) *Revolution in the Head: The Beatles' Records and the Sixties.* London: Vintage.

- McCartney, P. and Miles, B. (1998) *Paul McCartney: Many Years From Now.* London: Vintage.

- Norman, P. (2009) *John Lennon: The Life.* New York: HarperCollins.

- Norman, P. (2017) *Paul McCartney: The Biography.* London: Weidenfeld & Nicolson.

- Stark, S.D. (2006) *Meet the Beatles: A Cultural History of the Band that Shook Youth, Gender and the World.* New York: HarperCollins.

- Turner, S. (2015) *The Complete Beatles Songs.* London: Carlton Books Limited.

- Turner, S. (2016) *Beatles '66; The Revolutionary Year.* New York: HarperCollins.

FILMS AND DOCUMENTARIES

- *A Hard Day's Night.* (1964) [Film]. Richard Lester. Dir. UK: Walter Shenson Films.

- *Help!* (1965) [Film]. Richard Lester. Dir. UK: Walter Shenson Films, Subafilms.

- *The Beatles Anthology.* (1995-1996) [Documentary series]. Neil Aspinall and Chips Chipperfield. Producers. UK: Apple Corps, Capitol Records, Granada Television.

COMMEMORATIVE BUILDINGS

- In Liverpool:

  - There are guided tours of places where the Beatles spent time, or which are mentioned in their songs, including Penny Lane, the Cavern Club and Lennon and McCartney's childhood homes.
  - The Beatles Story, a museum dedicated to the group and located at the Albert Dock, opened in 1990.
  - The city's airport was renamed Liverpool John Lennon Airport in 2002.
  - In 2015, bronze statues of the four members

of the group by the sculptor Andy Edwards were unveiled on the banks of the River Mersey.

- In Hamburg:

  - The Beatles-Platz, located near the clubs where the group played between 1960 and 1962, was officially opened in September 2008.
  - At the centre of the Beatles-Platz there are five statues representing John Lennon, Paul McCartney, George Harrison, Pete Best and Stuart Sutcliffe, the lineup of the band when they played in Hamburg.

- Elsewhere:

  - There are statues and museums dedicated to the Beatles in many other locations around the world, including Russia, the USA, Italy, Poland, Peru and Mongolia.
  - The four Beatles each have two stars on the Hollywood Walk of Fame in Los Angeles –

one for their work as part of the group, and one for their respective solo careers.

ICONOGRAPHIC SOURCES

- The Beatles at New York's John F. Kennedy International Airport, 7 February 1964. Royalty-free reproduction picture.

- Vinyl of *Introducing… The Beatles* (1964), the first Beatles album released in the USA. Royalty-free reproduction picture.

- John Lennon and Yoko Ono in Amsterdam, March 1969. © Joost Evers/Anefo.

- Cover of the White Album, 1968. Royalty-free reproduction picture.

50MINUTES.com

History

Business

Coaching

Book Review

Health & Wellbeing

IMPROVE YOUR GENERAL KNOWLEDGE

IN A BLINK OF AN EYE !

www.50minutes.com

Although the editor makes every effort to verify the accuracy of the information published, 50Minutes.com accepts no responsibility for the content of this book.

© 50MINUTES.com, 2018. All rights reserved.

www.50minutes.com

Ebook EAN: 9782808006767

Paperback EAN: 9782808007856

Legal Deposit: D/2018/12603/13

Cover: © Primento

Digital conception by Primento, the digital partner of publishers.